D1287830

# Boa Constrictors

## By Sam Dollar

## STECK-VAUGHN
ELEMENTARY · SECONDARY · ADULT · LIBRARY

A Harcourt Company

www.steck-vaughn.com

ANIMALS OF THE RAIN FOREST

Library of Congress Cataloging-in-Publication Data is available upon request.

Printed and bound in the United States of America
10 9 8 7 6 5 4 3 2 1 W 04 03 02 01


**Photo Acknowledgments**
Corbis/, 16, 19, 20, 22
Unicorn Stock Photos/Ted Rose, cover
Visuals Unlimited/Joe McDonald, title page, 4-5, 8, 11, 24;
    Jim Merli, 12, 14; John Cunningham, 26; W. Ormerod, 28

# Contents

MEXICO

BELIZE
HONDURAS

GUATEMALA
EL SALVADOR

NICARAGUA

Caribbean
Sea

COSTA RICA

PANAMA

ECUADOR

COLOMBIA

VENEZUELA

North
Atlantic
Ocean

GUYANA
SURINAME

FRENCH
GUIANA
(FRANC

PERU

AMAZON
RIVER

BRAZIL

BOLIVIA

South
Pacific
Ocean

PARAGUAY

CHILE

South
Atlantic
Ocean

ARGENTINA

URUGUAY

Range of the
Boa Constrictor

Surrounding
Land

Water

N
W E
S

Borders

Rivers

# A Quick Look at Boa Constrictors

**What do boa constrictors look like?**

Boa constrictors are cream colored, brown, red, or gray snakes. They have dark brown to deep red-brown markings. A marking is a pattern on an animal. The markings get wider and darker near the tail.

**Where do boa constrictors live?**

Many boa constrictors live in the Central and South American rain forests. They also live in Mexico and Argentina.

**What do boa constrictors eat?**

Boa constrictors eat other animals. They eat lizards, rats, mice, pigs, squirrels, and birds. Larger boa constrictors may eat small deer.

This is a close-up view of a boa constrictor's scales.

# About Boa Constrictors

Boa constrictors are **reptiles**. A reptile is a **cold-blooded** animal that crawls or creeps. The blood in cold-blooded animals warms or cools to about the same temperature as the air or water around them. Temperature is a measure of heat or cold. Boa constrictors warm their bodies by lying in the sun. They cool their bodies by lying in the shade.

Like all reptiles, tough **scales** cover boa constrictors. Scales are parts of skin that lay over each other. They are made out of material called keratin. People's fingernails are made of the same material as a boa constrictor's scales.

## Where Boa Constrictors Live

Boa constrictors live in different **habitats**. A habitat is a place where an animal or plant usually lives. Some boa constrictors live in dry parts of Mexico and Argentina. Many live in the rain forests of South and Central America. Rain forests are places where many trees and plants grow close together and much rain falls. The Amazon rain forest is the largest rain forest in the world. It grows around the Amazon River in South America. Many different kinds of animals live in rain forests.

Boa constrictors live in different places in the rain forest. Young boa constrictors will climb trees. Adult boa constrictors crawl along the ground. They also spend time near rivers and streams.

## What Boa Constrictors Look Like

Boa constrictors are large snakes. Females grow larger than males. The average boa constrictor adult is from 6 to 11 feet

**This boa constrictor is crawling out of a river in the rain forest.**

(1.8 to 3.4 m) long. It weighs about 30 pounds (13.6 kg).

Boa constrictors are cream colored, brown, red, or gray with dark brown markings. A marking is a pattern on an animal. The markings get wider and darker toward the tail.

Over time, boa constrictors have changed to fit in with their environment.

# Crawling

Boa constrictors use large scales called **scutes** to travel on land. Scutes cover the underside of a boa constrictor. They push and pull themselves along by pressing scutes into the ground.

Boa constrictors also have spurs. Spurs are small bones that stick out near the tail. They are like claws. Scientist think these spurs are what is left of leg bones. They think that boa constrictors may once have had legs.

Boa constrictor skeletons have bones that look like pelvis bones and leg bones. Scientists think these bones show that boa constrictors have changed over time. The scientists think the boa constrictors changed as their environment changed. This helped them live better in changing habitats.

Some boa constrictors open their mouths when they are about to attack.

# Hunting and Eating

Boa constrictors are carnivores. Carnivores are animals that eat only other animals. Boa constrictors eat lizards, rats, mice, squirrels, and birds. Larger boa constrictors will eat small deer and ocelots. Ocelots are small, spotted wild cats that also live in the rain forest.

Boa constrictors can live a long time without food. Large boa constrictors can go months between meals. This is helpful when food is hard to find.

Boa constrictors quietly sneak up on prey that they want to eat.

## Hunting

Boa constrictors are predators. Predators are animals that eat other animals. The animals that predators eat are called prey. Boa constrictors often wait quietly in trees or bushes for prey. Because they blend in with trees and grass, they are hard to see.

Boa constrictors sometimes sneak up on prey. They will climb trees to catch birds or other animals. They will crawl into holes in the ground to find prey.

A boa constrictor strikes when it finds prey. Strike means it shoots forward with its mouth open. Then it sinks its teeth into the prey. It wraps its body around the animal while its teeth hold the prey.

Boa constrictors' teeth curve backwards. They keep prey from pulling out. The teeth sink deeper when prey tries to get free.

Boa constrictors kill their prey by squeezing tightly. They hold prey so tight that it cannot breathe. The prey's blood stops flowing. After a few minutes, it dies.

Many people say that boa constrictors crush the bones of their prey. This is not true. They only squeeze hard enough so the prey cannot breathe.

# Eating

Boa constrictors have special jaws that open very wide. They swallow their prey whole. In the roof of a boa constrictor's mouth is a group of **cells** called **Jacobson's organ**. A cell is a small part of an animal or plant. Boa constrictors press their tongues against Jacobson's organ to help them smell and taste.

Swallowing large prey takes a long time. The boa constrictor's mouth slowly works its way around the prey. Then muscles inside the throat grip the prey. These muscles push the prey to the stomach.

Strong stomach juices help boa constrictors digest bones and beaks of prey. To digest is to break down food so the body can use it. A small lizard can be digested in a few days. A larger animal can take more than two weeks to digest. A boa constrictor has a lump in its body until the prey breaks down.

> **Boa constrictors open their mouths wide to swallow prey.**

The outside temperature controls how fast a boa constrictor can break down food. The boa constrictor breaks down food more slowly in cool weather. That is why the cold-blooded boa constrictors might have to lie in the sun after eating. The heat helps them break down food faster.

Boa constrictors spend most of their lives on their own. .

# Life Cycle

Boa constrictors mate once a year. They live alone and come together only during the mating season. Females give off special scents to attract males. After mating, the male boa constrictor goes off on his own.

Female boa constrictors do not lay eggs like most reptiles. The young grow inside the female for 6 to 10 months. Then, females give birth to live young. Large female boa constrictors give birth to up to 50 young at a time.

This adult boa constrictor has few enemies in its natural habitat.

## Egg Sac

A thin and clear egg sac covers newly born boa constrictors. A sac is an animal or plant part that is shaped like a bag. Most young boa constrictors break through the sac easily. They will die if they cannot break out.

Young boa constrictors can be up to 2 feet (.6 m) long at birth. The length of young boa constrictors depends largely on the length of the mother. Longer females usually give birth to longer young.

## On Their Own

Female boa constrictors leave right after their young are born. Young boa constrictors must care for themselves. They have to hunt for food. They must hide from predators without the help of their mothers.

Only a few boa constrictors will become adults. Many die after a few weeks because birds, wild pigs, and other snakes eat them. They are not large enough or strong enough to fight back. If they grow larger, they will have few enemies.

This is the shed skin of a boa constrictor after molting.

# Molting

Like all snakes, a boa constrictor gets too big for its skin as it grows. New skin begins to grow underneath the old skin. They shed their old skins when they grow. This is called **molting**. Snakes shed skin, but do not shed scales.

Molting begins when a boa constrictor's new skin underneath is fully grown. They may rub against a rock to help loosen the old skin. The old skin peels back as the snake crawls out of it.

Boa constrictors grow throughout their lives. As they grow, they have to molt again and again. Boa constrictors can live for 30 to 40 years.

This is an ancient Aztec statue of a boa constrictor.

# Life with Boa Constrictors

In early times, the Aztec and Maya Indians of Central America believed boa constrictors and other snakes were gods. They thought these snakes could help bring rain for their crops. They carved huge boa constrictors out of stone to honor the snakes.

Christopher Columbus landed in the West Indies in 1492. He and his explorers went back to England and told stories of giant monsters. They said these monsters were hundreds of feet long and could swallow elephants. They did not know that what they really saw were boa constrictors and other large snakes.

 **Boa constrictors are popular pets.**

## Stories

People no longer ask boa constrictors to help bring rain, but they still tell stories. One of these stories is that boa constrictors crawl faster than a person can run. This is not true. Boa constrictors move slowly. Another story is that boa constrictors kill and swallow many people each year. This also is not true. They do not grow large enough to eat people.

## Boa Constrictors as Pets

Boa constrictors have become popular pets. They are very quiet and like to stay still much of the time. They do not make noises. They do not need to be fed very often. They do not need a lot of space.

Owners of boa constrictors need to be careful. Many large boa constrictors will strike at any sudden movement. They can eat cats and dogs. Owners of boa constrictors can be bitten.

## In the Wild

There are many boa constrictors living in the wild. They are not listed as endangered. Endangered means in danger of dying out.

People who buy and sell boa constrictors as pets must obey laws. Without laws, the buying and selling of boa constrictors would probably increase. The laws help make sure that boa constrictors will not die out.

# Glossary

**cell** (SEL)—a small part of an animal or plant

**cold-blooded** (kohld-BLUHD-id)—animals with blood that warms or cools to about the same temperature as the air or water around them

**habitat** (HAB-i-tat)—the place where an animal or plant usually lives

**Jacobson's organ** (JAYK-ub-suns OR-gun)—a group of cells in a boa constrictor's mouth that helps it taste and smell

**molt** (MOHLT)—to shed an outer skin or covering

**reptile** (REP-tile)—a cold-blooded animal that crawls or creeps

**scale** (SKAYL)—a small piece of thick, hard skin

**scute** (SKYOOT)—a large scale an animal uses to pull itself along on the ground

# Internet Sites

**Herp-Edia**
http://www.herp-edia.com

**Reptiles Park**
http://www.reptilespark.com

**The Snake.org**
http://www.thesnake.org

# Useful Addresses

**Minnesota Herpetological Society**
10 Church Street SE
Minneapolis, MN 55455-0104

**West Texas Herpetological Society**
P.O. Box 60134
San Angelo, TX 76906

# Index